God's "Holydays" Through the Seasons

*To Helen
Keep on Trusting,
loving the Lord
Peggy Hagoski*

Peggy Hagoski

Illustrations by Anne Spaulding

God's "Holydays" Through the Seasons

Copyright © 2010 Peggy Hagoski. All rights reserved. No part of this book may be reproduced or retransmitted in any form or by any means without the written permission of the publisher.

Published by Wheatmark®
610 East Delano Street, Suite 104, Tucson, Arizona 85705 U.S.A.
www.wheatmark.com

ISBN: 978-1-60494-264-4
LCCN: 2009930784

Acknowledgements

I want to thank, first of all, the Lord Jesus Christ for giving me an opportunity to write for Him. He gets all the glory! Many thanks to Kari Czer for her encouragement, without which this book would never have come into existence. For her patience and insight in putting it together, may God reward her. Thanks to my wonderful family for giving me support, inspiration, and love to be able to write.

"The Sovereign Lord is my strength, He makes my feet like the feet of a deer, He enables me to go on the heights."

Contents

Winter

Christmas

Truth Beckons 13
The Christmas Within 14
Just for Children 15
Gift Wrapped! 16
Let Truth Prevail 17
Gifts for Jesus 18
The Best Gift Yet 19
God's Best Gift Isn't… 20
The Perfect Gift 21
A Star Is Born 22
Isaiah 9:6-7 24
Jesus the Son 25

The Main Event 26
Christmas in the City 27

Hannukkah
Light Another Candle 31

New Year's Day
Your Point of View 35
Anchors Aweigh for a New Year 36
The Art of Traveling in a New Year. . . . 37
Gifts for a New Year 39

Valentine's Day
My Lovely Valentine 43
I Love You 44

President's Day
Our Presidents 47
Two Great Men 48

Spring
Ah Spring 51
Springtime 52
New Life 53

Resurrection Day

Bulletin.	55
A Time to Die and Rise Again.	57
The Mighty Conqueror	58
But, He Arose.	59
The Resurrection Day Triumph.	60
The Empty Tomb.	61
A Love Affair.	62
God Had a Plan!	63
If I Were God	64
He's Alive!.	65
But After the Third Day...	66
Christ Lives!.	67

Mother's Day

A Treasure.	71
Another Name for Mother	72
Mother's Lessons.	73
She's Special.	74
My First Love.	75
A Mother's Prayers.	76
I.O.U. MOM.	77
A Good Steward	78
Blessed is the Mother.	79
My Mother's Garden.	80

Memorial Day

God Remembers 83
A Memorial Day Tribute 84
May I Not Forget 85

Father's Day

My Wonderful Dad 89
Father Knows Best 90
The Irreplaceable Dad 91
A Dad Has to Learn 92
Dad's off His Tractor 93
On Shifting Sand 94
My Dad 95
Father and Son 96
My Heritage 97
Close to Perfection 98
My Dream 99

Summer

Hello Summer 103
Summer Sounds I Like Best 104
When God Smiles 105

Independence Day

Celebrating the Fourth 109
A Holy Day Gift 110
The Ultimate Freedom 111

It's for Freedom 112
Our Flag Is Still There 113
Liberty throughout the Land 114
Dear Lord... 115
The Declaration of Independence. 116
Mission Accomplished 117

Labor Day

Labor Day 121
A Labor Day Rest 122
God's Laborers 123
A Labor Day Reminder 124
In His Vineyard 125

Autumn

A Father's Promise 129
Good Bye Summer 130
It's Fall!. 131

Thanksgiving

Thanksgiving Virtue 135
Dear Lord 136
Give Thanks to God! 137
Thankful? 138
A Season of Thanksgiving 139
Happy Thanksgiving, Lord 140
Happy Thanksgiving. 141

I'll Always Thank Him. 142
Thank You, Lord 143
Mr. Turkey. 144

Truth Beckons

The angel came to Mary
To tell her she'd conceive
A baby who would be God's Son,
If she would but believe.

The angels came to shepherds
Upon Judean hills,
Men unwashed and dirty
Bereft of jewels and frills.

The wise man, too, were alerted
By the star they saw in the east;
They believed enough to follow
From the greatest of them to the least!

But no angel came to Pilate,
Nor to the great high priest,
Not to Herod in his palace
With his royal robes and feasts

Truth will never beckon
The haughty or the proud,
Whose minds resist the truth
And whose hearts refuse to bow.

The Christmas Within

Mary believed in God all of her life
She was young and single, not any man's wife.
Humble and pure a most dutiful maid,
Looking to God for needs when she prayed.

Her faith was so strong and her conscience clear,
She walked with her God having nothing to fear.
But when Gabriel came with the news of God's Son,
It troubled her to know how this thing could be done.

Knowing she was a virgin and never was wed,
She chose to believe what the angel had said,
Of all maidens she was the one to be favored
She marveled and rejoiced in God... now her Savior!

The miraculous comes to those who receive
The Jesus within that God wants to conceive.
So he can show his mercy and grace
To the blind who are longing to see his face!

Just for Children

Christmas is just for children they say,
I concur with those words of the wise.
If you want to be touched by joy,
You must see through a small child's eyes.

To believe in the wonder of Jesus,
The Savior who came to this earth,
You have to be open and trusting
To accept the fact of His birth.

Christmas is only for children?
Why, the shepherds were touched by the light,
The wisemen were lost in awe,
At that unique, glorious night!

If Christmas is only for children,
Then let innocent trust interrupt,
My life over and over again
And may I never grow up!

Gift Wrapped!

When Mary gave birth to Jesus that day
She'd no idea how this would affect everyone.
She wrapped him snug and warm in swaddling clothes,
What a precious gift from heaven, God's Son.

He didn't come clothed in purple satins and silks.
Nor in a palace with marble columns of white.
But he linked himself with frail humanity
And identified with our fallen state plight.

The Jews had been looking for a Messiah
To conquer the Romans and set them free.
But Jesus came to set up his own kingdom,
Independent of any military siege.

The whole world would receive a fresh vision of God
Giving the words: compassion and love, a face.
Pulling back the veil of secrecy from their eyes.
Giving freely the gift of his mercy and grace!

Let Truth Prevail

I love the warm and fuzzy feelings of Christmas
I love the lights in the windows downtown,
The hustle and bustle of the season
Makes my heart sing and my world go round.

Santas all dressed up in red costumes
Make a picture of festive inspiration,
Warming the hearts of the little ones
Who wait in happy anticipation.

But the lights will go out and trees come down
Then as the season and good feelings fade,
The hustle and bustle comes to an end
And we'll go back to the daily parade.

Fantasy is fun, but truth will prevail,
The season is here because of God's Son.
He lights up the world, destined he came,
Offering His peace: great joy and love has begun!

Gifts for Jesus

'Twas the night before Christmas and under the tree,
There were gifts wrapped for Jesus and all were from me.
There's nothing He needs and all that He's asked
Is a heart that is humble and fit for his task.
It's me that needs changing and this Christmas I'll give,
All the things that'll please Him for the life that I live.
So, I've wrapped up confession, it cleanses the soul,
Commitment, obedience, and yes, self-control.
Praise, adoration and gratitude's a good start
Love that's unending and straight from the heart.
Forgiveness and mercy, hard things to let go,
But, with the armor of God, I can defeat every foe.
Unwavering faith, self-denial, godliness
Hard things to give, but he does esteem holiness.
The key to them all is in the box tied with my love,
It will unlock every present above.

The Best Gift Yet

December with its wintry blasts,
Snowy trees long shadows cast.
Cheery fires, cozy homes
Parents reading Christmas poems.

Presents by the Christmas tree,
Children waiting anxiously.
Smallest gifts make eyes grow wide,
Wanting so to peek inside.

Mother and dad scurrying around,
Last minute chores still to be found.
Santas coming with bigger toys,
Parents tell their girls and boys.

But from heavens lofty heights,
Comes one who has the gift of life.
No more waiting for this present,
Invite Him in and feel his presence!

God's Best Gift Isn't...

All the worthless tinsel
We hang upon the tree
Nor the bright, colored lights
For on-lookers to see.

It isn't
The pretty wrapped presents
That inspire ooh's and aah's
The toys and the glitter
That give the children pause.

It isn't
Santa whom we feed with
Large Christmas cookies.
Stockings hung be the fire
With peppermint goodies.

It is ...
The mystery of all times
Made known and now begun
It's the most Unspeakable,
Wonderful, Jesus, Gods Son!

The Perfect Gift

I want to tell you of a gift and what it means to me,
How it brought such peace and rest and perfect harmony.
Your credit card is useless as far as this gift's concerned.
Don't climb the corporate ladder for the gift cannot be earned.
The grocery store, forget it, you can't use cash and carry
The supermart won't stock it even if the boss you marry
You can call your broker, but Wall Street hasn't heard,
And they'll trade anything from the ridiculous to the absurd!
Neiman Marcus, Saks and I. Magnin all cater to the elite.
They may have fascinating things, but my gift can't be beat!
You can look in all the malls and shop until you drop,
You'd never find this gift even if you shopped and shopped and shopped!
You could gorge yourself on goodies and put on weight with sweets,
But this won't bring the gift to you no matter what you eat.
Let me share with you a secret that if you should take a poll,
You'd find nothing that can fulfill the longings of the soul.
But Jesus can for He's the gift who turned my life around,
Sin and sorrow had to flee when this perfect gift I found!

A Star Is Born

He was...a young star in the cosmic space
Tiny in the firmament throng
Hidden behind the brighter lights
Of stars more powerful and strong

He felt useless and neglected
Forever doomed to travel the sky
In the course that God had ordered,
Never to complain or question why.

One day the Master Producer gave
A casting call to all His Galaxies
No experience would be needed,
To alter the course of history.

The little star yearned to be useful,
But how could he with light so dim?
So he continued in his orbit,
Until the Master noticed him.

"Come, little one you'll be the star
That will shine brighter than the sun
Some wisemen will need a light to
Help them to find my one and only Son!"

This gaseous, luminous glow
Gave his consent to play a role,
Affecting every human being
Reaching deep into the soul.

Heaven rang with joyous laughter,
Mary gazed at her treasure and smiled,
As this bright, new Star of Bethlehem
Shone down on the little Christ Child.!

Isaiah 9:6-7

Long ago in ancient times
A prophecy was written
"Unto us a child is born
To us a Son is given"

That prophecy came true we know
Two thousand years ago.
That baby boy was born on earth
In spite of many a foe.

His names were placed upon that scroll
See Isaiah nine, verse six and seven.
He's called Wonderful, Counselor,
The promised deity from heaven.

Acknowledge Him, praise and adore
This mighty God in human likeness
For Love came down to rescue us
And the gift He gives is priceless!

Jesus the Son

Church bells ring
Christmas is here
Children all sing
But where is the cheer?

Put aside cares
Worry and stress,
Come to the Savior
Bring your distress.

Sit at His Feet,
Feel His cool touch,
Here, is the peace
You thirst for so much.

The joy's in the season
And the joy's in the fun
Because of the person
Of Jesus the Son!

The Main Event

Christmas is not the story of Mary,
The wisemen were not heaven sent.
The shepherds were ordinary people,
Jesus is the main event!

Those who followed the star
Came to worship the Holy One,
And Mary and Joseph looked on in awe
At seeing God's only Son.

He came to seek and to save,
Those who truly believed in their hearts
Bowing down in humble behavior,
Realizing their need for the Wonderful Savior.

Christmas in the City

Christmas for sale, a little shop worn
The edges are tattered, all torn.
There in the warehouse from some shopping mall,
Shepherds are kneeling with no sheep to call.

Angels stand silent, they speak not a word,
No glorious message from on high can be heard.
Dusty old wisemen with their star from the east,
Looking tired and dirty stacked up in a heap.

So tender and mild, Joseph, Mary and the manger,
The Baby missing, purloined by a stranger.
The birth of the Christ Child born in a stable,
Now declared a tall tale, somebody's fable.

Some merchants wait for the day they call Christmas
Their only interest is the money and big business.
And now, it's out with the old and on with the new,
Being godly is something the ignorant do.

A witness for Christ is seldom or never heard.
"God Bless you," is deemed only out dated words.
These stories of Jesus are truths still received,
For it will always be Christmas in hearts not deceived.

Hannukkah

Light Another Candle

All over the world candles are lit at sunset
It is Hanukkah the Jewish celebration,
Stirring up memories of a Temple long ago
Of the Maccabees and rededication.

For eight consecutive days lights are candled
To remember God's glory and powerful aura.
How he delivered them from their enemies
Symbolized by the lights of the Menorah.

Throughout the whole world is good times and bad,
Celebrations go on with gifts given, big and small,
Enjoyed with food that commemorates the event
That takes them, for a moment to the Western Wall.

God never rejects His people whom He foreknew.
There were the patriarchs and Abraham, His friend,
With whom He made an everlasting covenant.
For the faithful, God's miracles will never end.

New Year's Day

Your Point of View

Dear Lord,
I'll definitely need help this coming year.
When I'm confused and don't know what to do.
I can get very uncooperative and stubborn
And forget to seek your point of view.

You have said,"Take pleasure in reproaches,
In persecution, hardships, loss and distress."
Help me to see the opportunity for growth,
And gladly accept your viewpoint of stress.

Help me to see that things work together
For the good of all who truly love you.
When you have my best interest at heart
How can I be afraid of your point of view?

When I am weak, then in you, I am strong.
In the stillness of my pain you come through
For then you are able to change my heart,
So I can see things through your point of view.

Then I'll not be afraid of the darkness,
Knowing you'll know what I'm to do,
Just keep reminding me day after day
That I really can rely on your point of view!

Anchors Aweigh for a New Year

A ship in a harbor is enchanting indeed
With sails caught tightly to mast,
Held by the anchor so firm and snug
To the dock safely tied up fast.

But a ship is not built to be snug in a slip,
It is meant to be out in the blow.
To roll and to toss in the cavernous sea,
By the storms that will come and go!

There'll be times of calm to just drift along
When the turbulent waters cease.
But be it quiet or rough on a bumpy course,
The Captain, Himself, is your peace.

So, Anchors aweigh, cast off, set your course
Give the Pilot full charge in the gale.
Let the winds and the waves take you wherever
The Master thinks fit for the sail!

The Art of Traveling in a New Year

I'm setting out on a new journey
To places that I've never been before.
New territories that I'd heard about
And the time has come for me to explore.

Although I'm somewhat apprehensive
I have a personal helper by my side.
If I'm nervous he'll calm my fears
So that I can settle down and enjoy the ride

I must have faith in His ability
He has the minutest detail all worked out.
And if I obey His rules of the road,
Then things will go smoother en route.

The first rule of the road is not to look back
In despair of the tasks I've left behind.
Some nostalgia is okay, but no regrets
For traveling light is the best way I find.

Another rule is to be patient with others.
There will be difficult people on board.
To be respectful is what the Guide asks,
And there'll be trouble if he is ignored.

I may get restless and bored with the view
When what God created is not to my liking,

My Guide knows when to discipline,
And, a mountain appears and we go hiking!
I'm traveling this New Year with anticipation,
For the Lord and I have adventures to share.
I've a wrinkle or two that a hot iron will fix,
And I'm letting Him worry about the wear and tear.

Gifts for a New Year

Remember the gifts you received at Christmas time?
All wrapped in pretty paper, you were excited.
Some were a puzzle, but you were gracious,
Others were special and you were delighted.

Gifts are given with good intentions,
Someone cared enough to think things through.
A friend planned and looked forward to the day
To give you a gift that would surely please you!

The things we value on the earth are temporary.
They may wind up in the attic stored in a trunk.
But compared with what God has to offer,
They are transitory dust that some would call junk.

The Father is waiting to give you presents.
Some gifts may perplex you, I'm sure.
But others can be the desires of your heart,
The very thing you've longed and prayed for.

God has planned your future since the beginning,
His thoughts toward you are like diamonds in a mine.
He eagerly awaits to give you His blessings,
And to portion them out in this New Year of thine.

Valentine's Day

My Lovely Valentine

You are my light that scatters darkness.
You illuminate truth for me to share
You swallow up my weak resistance,
Your love envelops me, You are there!

Sometimes like a small light on the wall,
You keep me from stumbling in the dark
From little dangers that would wound me
During the night you are my Hallmark.

You are the sensor that lights up my way,
But until it's needed it does not shine.
When I face the darkness and grope along
Suddenly, you show yourself, You are mine!

You are my beacon to warn me just in time,
Keeping me from the rocks along the shore.
Flashing across my deep and trackless sea
I'm never lost, your presence is secured.

You are sometimes like the sun to me,
Flooding my soul with your intense light.
The evidence of you overwhelms me,
Gives me great assurance, You are my life!

I Love You

Can you fathom how God gives His love
Without measure to every creature?
And it's given without any strings
An essential part of His nature.

More copious when He's correcting
For He knows you'll need it more then.
Love that steadies and stays His hand,
Shows Him exactly how much and when

His tears always fall with your tears,
And when your learning time is through,
He gathers you up in His great big arms,
And continually says, "I love You!"

Remember God's love is unconditional,
For around the world it's been heard
He will never turn His back on you
For He cannot go back on His Word!

President's Day

Our Presidents

We pay tribute to all of our presidents,
We've set aside a day of remembrance.
To recognize their sacrificial giving,
Serving country and pledging their allegiance.

In God's great foresight, wisdom and grace,
He knew that freedom was going to be tough,
He chose dedicated men of honor and potential,
Not all believers but diamonds in the rough.

All were appointed and sanctioned by God,
Being set aside to carry out His plan.
There is no authority but what He allows,
Established by Him and not mere man.

Orderly governments are God's provision,
Until Christ returns according to plan.
He has delegated those in authority,
Representing the Good Shepherd who is
The Great I AM.

Two Great Men

God blessed our country and I'm the biggest fan,
Of two special men who lived and loved this land.

Called by Almighty God to serve in the front lines,
Willingly giving of their time and their lives.

Didn't require a lot of education or might
Just to trust in Him wholly and follow His light.

They had many struggles and burdens to bear.
But God heard their cries and met with them there.

Washington and Lincoln were two brave men,
Chosen by the Creator to do a great work,
And I say Amen!

Ah Spring

A fading out of winter scenes.
Grasses growing rich and green.
Hilltops wearing a tiara of lace.
Warm winds blow, melting crowns cascade.

New life bursting all around,
Flowers peeking through the ground.
Trees sport showy buds and leaves.
Birds in flight soar high and free.

Spring's arrived and summer's not far.
Nature's clothed in her colorful garb.
Change is the way it needs to be,
For our God is a God of variety!

Springtime

I love the look of Springtime
The trees are dressed in their new, green suit.
It's a transformation from death to life.
Every seed, bulb and plant will take root.

I find there is hope in the Springtime.
The crocus and lily dance in the breeze.
Newness of life can be found everywhere
Birds will soon take on a family to feed.

There is excitement in the Springtime.
Brides plan elaborate weddings for June.
Spring fever is catching, it's in the air
Grooms can't escape for love is in bloom!

There is great comfort in the Springtime.
Hopes that have lain dormant will come true.
In our Springtime, God will reawaken us
From our winter solstice and make all things new.

New Life

Wintertime is almost over.
Earth shakes off its feeling of gloom.
And once more spring comes forth
Awakening the ground to bloom.

Like a bride having dressed in white.
Now cloaks herself to alter the scene.
Celebrates with flowers in her hair.
Trading winter white for vibrant green.

Blossoms are calling to blossoms.
Leaves happily unfold and appear.
It's the loveliest time to be alive.
The most beautiful time of the year.

Faith is renewed in the springtime.
God hasn't forgotten his own.
His promises are as sure as the growth
We see all around us made known.

Faith is built up in the springtime.
God's love is made clear and increased.
As by his power to bring to new life
That which was thought to be deceased.

resurrection day

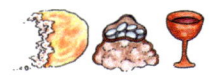

Bulletin

The whole town was a buzz with the news
The man they called Jesus had disappeared!
The chief priests and elders were adamant,
That the body had been stolen by his peers.

They spread the news in all Jerusalem
The grave was well guarded by soldiers.
Pilate made sure that the tomb was secure
And had the door sealed with a large boulder.

Jesus' friends were overcome with their grief
And as the women approached in their gloom,
They were startled to see an angel seated
Who told them, "There's no one here in this tomb."

"He has slipped out of his grave clothes
He has gone, He is risen just like He said.
He was crucified but now He is alive
This Jesus you seek has risen from the dead!"

The women, on their way to tell others
Were confused, afraid, wanting to believe
Then they saw Jesus and when He called them
They fell down in worship and clasped His feet.

Here was the Risen Lord right before their eyes,
He told them not to be troubled anymore.
For death and the grave could never hold Him.
The ransom had been paid, with good things in store.

The dreadful night had passed,. the battle was won.
He had been in hell and wrestled with Satan alone.
So prophecy was fulfilled and victory won.
And now He is alive to claim His rightful throne!

A Time to Die and Rise Again

Jesus came to earth with a purpose.
To atone for the sins of mankind.
He accomplished what was predicted
When in ignominy and shame he died.

He appeared as a man, but was fully God.
The women gathered to mourn their loss.
His heart bled for their pain and distress,
He could never prepare them for the cross.

Rulers looked on in stolid indifference,
Soldiers cast lots for his seamless garment.
The people were curious, but unmoved,
One thief saw the justice of his punishment.

He was on a mission greater by far
Than anyone could ever know or tell,
Before His Spirit departed from His body
He went down into the very depths of hell.

We only know the surface of His passion.
It's in the Spirit He conquered wicked foes.
When that was achieved He came up from the pit
And, with a victorious shout, He Arose!

The Mighty Conqueror

Jesus rose from the grave that early morn
A mighty conqueror over death and sin,
He did battle with the demons in hell
In a war Satan expected to win.

He struggled with the forces of evil,
Casting off the chains of oppression.
So we can live in the knowledge and
Fullness of the resurrection.

Nothing could keep Him in the tomb
Work was finished , mission achieved.
He rose up in victory and triumph,
With His Son, the Father was pleased.

He ascended on high with spoils of war.
We were buried with Him to arise
To participate in the the gifts He brought,
For He opened the door to Paradise!

Gifts of salvation and forgiveness
No longer servants and slaves of sin.
Gifts of knowing the Father in depth,
In a way never before given to men.

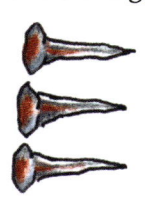

But, He Arose

He was a friend of sinners and beloved son.
This kind, gentle Jesus not raising a fist.
He healed the multitude, gave words of life,
And was betrayed by Judas with only a kiss

Believers were shaken as He hung on the cross
Faith stumbled in spirit at what this could mean.
Losing sleep, puzzled and saddened by the news,
Some fearfully hid so as not to be seen.

His death sent shock waves piercing Mary's heart.
The ground reeled, shook and trembled in dismay.
And with the sight of the Savior on the cross
The sun, moon and stars hid their light at midday.

He told them of His death and resurrection
They couldn't grasp the meaning of His story.
But as they believed they were enlightened
Seeing the miracle of heaven and all its glory.

But, HE AROSE. Victor over death and the grave.
A tangible, express image of His Father foretold.
Raised to bring new life and imparting to us
The experience and joy of heaven's threshold.

The Resurrection Day Triumph

While the world looks for bunnies,
Coloring eggs, fantasy and fun,
Resurrection Day is serious business,
It all has to do with God's Son.

Jesus looked weak as he hung on the cross,
Wickedness killed Him, it was their ploy.
Evil surrounded Him, hoping to win,
But He triumphed with shouts of pure joy!

The cross must come before victory.
Jesus must suffer, agonize and groan.
His life was torn from his broken body
Before satisfaction could come from the throne.

Satan thought he had him dead and buried.
Yet He was victorious and claimed his prize
Nothing could keep Him down in the grave,
He arose! He arose! He's alive!

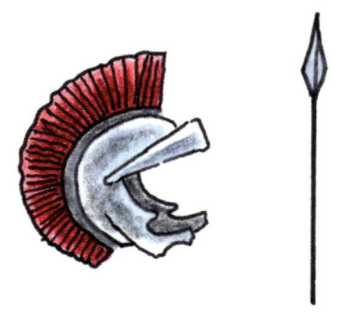

The Empty Tomb

It was early on that Sunday Morning
Some of the women went to the tomb
To anoint the body of Jesus,
With heavy hearts filled with gloom.

But all they saw were two angels,
Sitting alone in the empty place.
Mary said,"What have they done with my Lord?"
While tears ran down her sad face.

They could not comprehend, as yet.
Or understand what Jesus had said.
They had come to the tomb expecting
To see someone who surely was dead.

But He had shattered the evil forces,
His Resurrection Day had arrived,
He had opened the Holy of Holies
And to all who will receive Him...
He's Alive!!!!

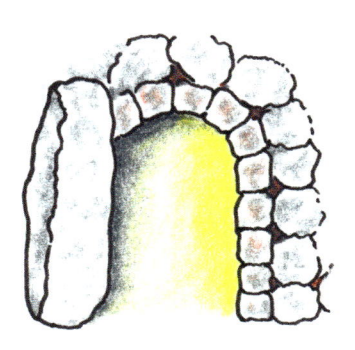

A Love Affair

He didn't count the cost nor
Figure up profit for loss.
He gave up His life in frailty,
A ransom for all humanity.

No romance on the silver screen,
No make-believe or foolish scheme.
He came to earth, His love to share,
For redemption is a love affair.

To die one might decide to end
One's life for a dear and trusted friend.
Yet, something in God's heart we find,
Transcends the gulf to all mankind.

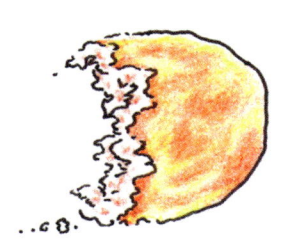

God Had a Plan!

Satan was on a mission,
To be like God was His plan.
To take over the universe
And govern the whole world and man.

But God's plan was best and true.
In Jesus, God showed His great power
For greater is He than Satan,
And the cross His successful hour.

His son died the cruelest of deaths.
And as He hung upon that tree,
Satan thought he had surely won,
And he clapped his hands in glee.

But the tomb had to give Him up.
And as angels stood 'round about,
He arose, the Mighty Conqueror
With a great triumphant shout!

If I Were God

If I were God
I couldn't send my son to the cross
To die in ignominy and shame.
To assuage the guilt and suffer
For mankind and take all the blame

If I were God
I couldn't stand to see him tortured
By noisy crowds cheering and jeering
As they crowned him in jest and fun,
His body bleeding, his flesh tearing.

If I were God
I wouldn't let my boy fight against
Spiritual forces in high places,
I would have taken on every evil
In Hell and all the heavenly spaces

But, God is God
He did it his own way, that is best.
Jesus endured the cross. God's own Son!
He went into the grave as a pauper
And he arose, the victory won!

He's Alive!

He allowed himself to be taken and bound,
Secretly convicted, "guilty as found."
He was the pure Lamb of God destined to die,
No defense or objection as his time drew nigh.

They nailed his hands and his feet to a cross.
Mary and others grieved for their loss.
They had not understood the words He had spoken,
All they knew was that their hearts were broken.

No one thought that He would be resurrected.
It was prophesied, but it wasn't expected.
They knew nothing of the battle that He would face,
Or the spiritual war for the whole human race.

He gave of himself because of God's grace.
Someone had to die and stand in our place.
He broke the curse and claiming his own
Made evil tremble as he took back his throne.

Soon miracles would turn grief into gladness.
For victory always takes away sadness.
He arose from the dead and what did He bring?
Riches and Glory befitting a King!

"Because He lives, we can live also"

But After the Third Day...

Why first the cross and not a throne?
Why betrayed, beaten and denied?
Why the agony of dying alone?
"Where are you my God?" he cried!

HE did it so our eyes could see
And behold God's unveiled face.
And our ears could hear and accept
His unspeakable, marvelous grace.

For the joy that was set before him
He gave up his life willingly.
None other had the power to do
What Jesus did for humanity.

In victory he arose from the grave.
New things he was ready to declare.
He sprang from the awful grasp of death,
Claiming his place as the rightful heir.

Christ Lives!

Judas sold him.
Stan mocked him.
Men reviled him.
As he hung on a tree.

The cross could not kill him.
The grave could not claim him.
Death could not decay him.
He lives for you and me.

All nature reveals him.
The heavens extol him.
Angels surround him.
He's alive, we're set free!

Mother's Day

A Treasure

There is a treasure in a human vessel.
My mother's was her faith in God.
She had a light that glowed within her
That shone like that of a goldenrod.

If you would want to meet her
She's not here anymore.
She's in heaven with Jesus
The one whom she always adored.

At times I "see" her so vividly.
The things she would do and say.
The way she leaned upon her God
Teaching me by example to pray.

If you could look in on her life,
You'd see her quietness and then,
How God used her weaknesses
To confound the wisdom of men.

Looking beyond her frailties,
And turning your gaze upon me
You'd see a very tiny replica
Of the way she used to be!

Why not take a moment from
Your busyness and things to do,
Listen to your heart and recall,
The things your mother did for you!

Another Name for Mother

She need not be an expert
In child psychology.
She only need to know that God
Knows all about perplexity.

She need never struggle
To reach God's expectations.
Nor would he condemn her
For her human limitations.

He has given her capacity
To love and nurture children.
For them she'd give her life.
She's a living, walking sermon.

As she puts her hand in God's,
And seeks to please none other,
Her offspring call her Blessed,
That's another name for Mother!

Mother's Lessons

Mother Learns:
To be patient in times of stress.
Knowing this too shall surely pass.
To discipline in love, not anger,
Is a victory that endures and lasts.

She Learns:
Time spent with God is essential.
She finds that prayer means power.
When problems arise she runs to Him
Knowing that He is her highest tower.

She Learns:
To manage her time and family
And not to look with envy next door
For cleaner, neater, smarter kids
And better prepared meals du jour.

She Learns:
How not to smother her precious one.
And to possess those she cannot own.
To be a parent, not a buddy
Rearing carefully, they're just on loan.

She Learns:
As the years go by there will be tears.
But joys will wash away those sorrows.
She sees that life is but a journey
And waits patiently for her tomorrows!

She's Special

You are very special in God's eyes.
Your hair, your eyes, your personality
Were all planned before earth's foundation.
He liked what He saw, you are a sensation.

He saw your family, your husband and kids.
Yes, and even a dog named Charlie.
Isn't it comforting to know about His plan?
And to know that He is your biggest fan?

He knew that you'd make a great mother.
He gave you wisdom to raise those children.
To have lots of grey matter in that lovely head
To keep the whole family in tact and well fed.

You make a home for the father of your brood.
Not one can take your place not even dad.
You share in creation, you are Abraham's seed.
You can know God as your friend, you are blesses indeed.

Your name is Mother and there is no one else.

My First Love

I want to tell you of a time
When I met my biggest fan.
Cheered on with love and hope
I became the person I am!

Some thought me rather ugly
But this person was satisfied.
The moment we were introduced
She cuddled me to her side.

When I felt afraid and lonely
In this strange and hostile place
Her quiet spirit calmed my fears
When she stroked my head and face.

I know I couldn't have made it
Without her special touch.
That unconditional love
Has shaped my life so much.

She always called me her angel
And her sweet and gentle dove.
I didn't know it at the time
But mother was my very first love.

A Mother's Prayers

The mother who puts her faith and trust in God,
Knowing that her prayers for her kids are sent
To the one who has understanding and knows
That a tree always grows as the twig is bent

But God specializes in unbending trunks
Who insist on going their own twisted way.
And a mother's prayers never return empty
Achieving great things as she continues to pray.

Many storms can come and damage the sapling.
And the root may not have enjoyed fertile ground
But God, being the wise and Master Gardener
Can salvage the tree making it healthy and sound.

Precious to him are the pleas of a mother.
He sees every heartache and tear drops that fall.
All that he asks is that she remain faithful
And keep believing that he'll take care of it all.

If God can send rain and snow upon the earth
Making it flourish and bud in its own time,
Then he can answer a mom's deepest yearning
And change a bent twig to grow straight as a pine..

I.O.U. Mom

I owe you, Mom, for many things.
I know I can't thank you enough.
With only "on the job" training
And no experience, that's tough.

I've forgiven you for all those lunches
When I ate tuna until I was blue.
Peanut butter is another sore spot.
But, then, what's a young mother to do?

I owe you, Mom, for the patience you had
In nursing me through colds and flu.
Kissing my every boo boo away
Healing knees and emotions too.

Thanks for all the little swats you gave
While it was still allowed at the time.
Didn't hurt me a bit except where I sit
And that has healed up just fine.

I wondered why you didn't pack and leave
When I cried and nagged all the while.
You'd send me to father to have OUR talk
When having a father was still in style.

How did you and God do it, this job of jobs
And not flip your proverbial lid?
You took a scrawny baby and turned me
Into a wonderful, fabulous kid!

A Good Steward

All that God required of a mother
Is that she be found faithful to her task.
She need not be a super woman
Dedication, is all he ever asks.

She man not care about farming or planting.
Nor canning her crop on a hot summer day.
But she cultivates her garden of offspring
Training them to grow straight and tall in God's way.

She may not have to work hard outside the home.
When she'd rather be a "stay at home mom."
Doing her best to help feed the family
She looks to the Lord to help keep her strong.

His foreknowledge God has given mothers
A love that endures whatever transpires.
The patience and stamina to keep going,
Courage to be the good steward he desires.

Blessed is the Mother

Blessed is the Mother
Whose God is the Lord
Who relies upon Him
And studies His Word

Who sets the example
Of a mother and wife
Through her actions of
Living a sanctified life.

Who looks to the Lord
For strength in her day
And fears not the storms
That may come her way.

Blessed is the Mother
Who walks in His ways,
No matter the path
Nor heat of the day.

Who's acquainted with God
Through Jesus the Son
And goes forth proclaiming
The Glorified One.

My Mother's Garden

My mother had a beautiful garden
She worked hard with her hands in the soil,
Enjoying the feel of the soft, dark earth,
And not afraid of the backbreaking toil.

She was acquainted with uninvited strangers
Who could wreak havoc with vegetation.
She fertilized, watered, weeded and kept watch
So the plants could grow to full maturation.

She knew that even in the Garden of Eden
A snake was just waiting for someone to fall.
Not any of her flowers would ever fall prey
To anything that could fly, hop walk or crawl.

Yes mother's garden was her prized possession.
A thing of value that was closest to her heart.
The garden that I speak of were her children
Planted there by God, His greatest work of art!

Memorial Day

God Remembers

I must run down to the mall today
They are having a wonderful event.
Why everything's priced at below cost
And more with the coupons they sent.

Memorial Day is the perfect day to shop
With my credit card convenient and near
There'll be zero percent finance charge
And I won't pay till next year!

I must remember to look at that dress
That appeared in the ad, it was so cute.
I saw the shoes that I've always wanted
They'd go perfect with my new blue suit.

I'm glad God keeps track of holidays
I'm no good at those things I regret.
So I'll just go shopping down at the mall
And have fun, relax and forget.

A Memorial Day Tribute

In Arlington National Cemetery,
Across the river from Washington DC
There lies the tomb of the Unknown Soldier
Being guarded by one pacing silently.

Today we pay tribute to all our heroes
Known and unknown, someone's girl, someone's boy.
They were courageous and gave all they had
To protect the freedom we now enjoy.

I will take the time to remember and give thanks
For those whose struggle with death meant liberation.
But the unfinished task is ever before us
As we continue the birthing of this great nation.

May I Not Forget

A Day of Remembrance is set aside
For Veterans who have died all over the world.
They were brave in serving God and country
Emotions are stirred when our flag is unfurled.

May the meaning of the day not be lost
In the clamor and clatter of an everyday thing,
When loneliness and anguish of families still echo
From the heart and soul of their being.

War has torn families apart for centuries.
Freedom's not built on greatness, glory or fame.
But on those whose future plans never came to be.
Those whose sacrifice gave liberty her name.

Sadly, it seems, there has been thoughtlessness
Of traditions and meaning of those who fall
Fewer parades or services, or graves looked after,
Perhaps distracted by a good time down at the Mall.

There's no "greater love" that one should die willingly
So others might live, this should earn our respect.
For those who have answered the highest call,
Are deserving of recognition not neglect!

God is acquainted with every woman and man
Who has died fighting for justice and for peace.
He's concerned over a bird that falls from the nest
His care for His creation will never cease.

Father's Day

My Wonderful Dad

What do I owe my Heavenly Father?
He has sent my dad to stand in His place
For a little one can't see or understand
The wonders of God's mercy and grace!

Someone to look up to and try to imitate
With the length and pace of a man's stride
Echoes and imitations of his dad's talk
Are heard as he chatters by his father's side.

He takes notice of his father's crooked smile
The way he stands up straight and tall.
How he follows the example before him
Will determine how he stands or falls.

A father is here by divine appointment!
All have the potential for being a dad
But only those who follow God's footsteps
Can truly be a real father to a little lad.

Father Knows Best

My father knows what's best for me.
He knows what makes me rich.
He holds me in his heart and mind
As I grow inch by inch.

He knows when I need discipline
And when my love grows cold.
He skims off all the dross to see
His reflection in the gold.

I may not think him fair at times
When I can't have my way.
But he sees the bigger picture
When I can only see today.

As I grow up into his image
And fit into his plans,
As he increases more and more,
I'll begin to understand.

My heavenly Father loves me so,
I've put him to the test.
I'm trusting him to see me through
For father always knows best.

The Irreplaceable Dad

After God had created heaven and earth
He did a lot of scouting around.
He selected some very good, rich earth
And sculptured something from out of the ground.

The angels gathered 'round as he worked
And asked, "God, is that what you call a man?"
And God replied, always willing to explain,
"Yes, it's to be a reflection of who I AM."

He'll have almost two hundred parts that move,
A brain to think and be very capable.
There'll be trouble in The Garden, for sure
But I've made him a tough individual.

He'll be able to discern the right from wrong
For The Fall brings enlightenment and misery.
I will send my Son to assuage my wrath for
My love includes a cure and remedy.

Sin will cast long shadows upon the earth
But I am the Light that outshines the sun.
My standards are high, but well within reach
For he's a facsimile of Me and my Son.

This man will be unique upon the whole earth.
He'll work hard to see that his family is clad.
No aunt, uncle, cousin, or even a mother
Can satisfy the heart of a child like a Dad!

A Dad Has to Learn

Just when a dad understands how to father
All the kids grow up and go out on their own.
But a father has to grow up and mature too
And a family is just the place to be honed.

A dad learns how to reflect God's image
Just as the moon reflects the light of the sun.
Even if no example was given to him
Or no father was around when he was young.

To grow, a dad goes through valleys and mountains.
He climbs every steep path and dangerous cliff.
Finds every toe-hold and hollow to hang onto
Aware of each stream whether slow or swift.

A dad has to learn to be a good listener.
How to handle each child with much gentleness.
He opens his heart and confesses his faults
To show them a glimpse of his humanness

He must recognize when his job is finished,
Just like the archer he pulls back the bow.
Sharpened and well equipped for the journey,
The arrow soars out when the archer lets go!

Dad's off His Tractor

A father used to plow, plant and sow.
He learned patience and waited for growth.
He'd feed the chickens, slop the hogs,
Curry the horse and chop up the logs.

When Sunday came, time to hitch up the horse.
The family in finery and as a matter of course.
They'd set off to church, old Dobbin knew the way,
And met with friends and neighbors to pray.

Dad has no need of a gym or a pool.
His strong physique came from working with tools.
Driving the tractor all day in the hot sun
Hour after hour until the work got done.

It's different now and things aren't the same.
Dad's on the freeway and not on the range.
The kids have to be picked up coming and going.
He's off his tractor (but still planting and sowing)

For a father is God's most necessary invention.
But, now other duties must claim his attention.
He's traded his farm for a "castle," and I might add,
He's the king of the house who we call Dad!

On Shifting Sand

Walk a little straighter daddy.
I can't follow if you don't leave
A clear and distinct footprint or
If you stumble, waver and weave.

Walk a little plainer daddy.
It's hard to hear you when you lead.
If your walk and your talk don't match,
To leave the pattern that I need
Walk a little closer daddy.
There's no one else to take your place.
Other steps are so confusing
For only you can set MY pace!

Walk a little clearer daddy.
So I can know just who I am.
Keep those footsteps firm and steady,
Because I walk on shifting sand!

My Dad

I dreamed a dream last night.
I had to pick out a dad.
There were so many choices
I was so confused and sad.

I saw all kinds, short and tall,
Thin and skinny, portly and stout.
Some were rich and well dressed,
Others in tatters walking about.

I looked them over one by one.
And even though I tried and tried
I was too young to choose a dad.
"Help me God," with tears I cried.

I wasn't given much time to observe
Or study each and every single one.
I quickly chose the one I thought
Could be my father and I his son.

As I slipped my small hand into his
I felt so nourished, this was my Dad!
When I awoke to my delight and joy.
I had picked the one I already had!

Father and Son

He was just a wee little tyke
Clinging to the hand of his dad.
Many people passed hurriedly by
Paying no attention to the lad.

The boy felt safety and contentment
Looking up at his father so strong.
A towering haven on that busy street
Nothing could ever harm or go wrong.

The man gazed down upon his offspring
Seeing there in his own reflection
Potential for future achievements
With pride, joy and filial affection.

The hand of the small one tightened,
Laughing together, they had such fun.
As the traffic kept rumbling near by
They were close as any father and son.

My Heritage

My father was a wonderful man.
Not perfect, but human as one could be.
He left a valuable heritage
Of faith and trust that he passed on to me..

I would know little of spiritual values
If I hadn't known that dad was on his knees.
Praying in times of great stress and anguish
To God, his friend, who always heard his pleas..

He not only prayed when storms engulfed..
But when life became peaceable and still.
For he knew that behind the ups and downs
Was the Father's mercy and perfect will..

That legacy will be with me forever.
Whether awake or asleep, it matters not.
I'll remember the spiritual lessons
Of wisdom dad left that can never be bought.

Close to Perfection

My dad's an ordinary sort of guy.
If you saw him you wouldn't say,
"Look, there goes a famous man or
An important person, per se."

He goes to his job day after day.
To keep his family together.
He struggles with the daily tasks,
But wears his load like a feather.

He asks for nothing in return,
But I'll give him appreciation.
I'll offer it freely because
He deserves all my adulation.

He's a stand-in for God to me.
A perfect example for any lad.
He's here by divine appointment
And I love him because he's my Dad!

My Dream

I dreamed that I was a Father.
The way was steep and hard.
No one was there to teach me
My steps were blurred and marred.

I expected perfect children
Who grow without attention.
I had to learn the hard way
In my pride and self-deception.

I didn't know that time was needed
To give that moment to hear and see
When excited children came to share,
But I was involved with only me!

I forgot to show my family
My weak and vulnerable side.
I never said "forgive my failings
I'm human, I erred, but I tried"

Had I shown more love to my wife
It would have been a positive move.
But I was set on being the boss
And our house became full of gloom.

I didn't know the children watched
To see what they should become.
I was not a good example
While their minds were like a sponge.

I thought that anger and shouting
Was the way to correct a child.
But discipline and love should go
Together when properly applied.

I took no thought for priority
To always put my family first.
And through my selfish motives
I lost what I loved the most.

I was awakened from my dream
Knowing God has every answer.
I'll follow Him and read His Word
For only He can make a Father!

Hello Summer

Where have you been for nine months?
We've missed you and we began to wonder.
I hear that you've been warming up other places
On the globe, such as, the land down under.

We're glad you're back we enjoy your company
Because you're a whole lot warmer than snow.
Can you stick around for more than three months?
Or do we have to settle for the afterglow?

Everything is so orderly in your world
You are only allowed to stay for a season
For the cycle must continue as God allows
Only in his own time, his own reason.

Autumn will soon be waiting in the wings.
Bringing with it a new perspective and plans.
So please don't mess with any circadian rhythm
Or there'll be confusion and a celestial jam!

Summer Sounds I Like Best

The barking of a dog in the distance.
The whisper of the wind in the trees.
The rain outside my window leaping
Down the drain, dripping from the eaves.

The mourning doves calling to each other
From the trees announcing their love tryst.
And the crackling of the telephone wires
In the dews and damps of the fog and mist.

Humming birds with a soft, high pitched whine
Carrying out their work with enthusiasm.
Taking quite seriously their daily tasks
While mocking birds vent their sarcasm.

Each sound gives praise to the Father above.
Earth moves and grows in a rhythm that lives.
The elements, the creatures are his works
All nature speaks of the life that he gives.

Above all the sweet sounds so gentle and soft
The rain, the birds singing in tranquil accord
The one I like best and that moves me the most
Is the still, small voice of my wonderful Lord!

When God Smiles

What if summer never came
No gentle rain for garlands
To water grass and flowers
And feed capricious gardens?

What if darkness still remained
To cloud the earth in gloom?
And summer with its radiance
Forgot to appear in June!

What if there were no birds
To test their brand new plumage?
No place for Robins to strut
No forests in which to forage?

But God has given us a season
With the fun and pleasure it brings.
For summer is the fulfillment
Of what was promised in the spring!

Thank God for this timely pause.
It's a sign of his love and care.
He graciously gives us a respite
As his smile once more warms the air!

Independence Day

Celebrating the Fourth

From the mountains, rivers, hills, and valleys
God has given America a big heart.
Because she stood up for freedom's way of life
It has been a country unique from the start.

God prepared the right soil to plant a nation
Long before the foundations of the earth was laid.
Then in his time and place a country grew
And was found in the balance and weighed.

Pleased with its equilibrium and equality
And satisfied with how it tipped the scales,
Bringing glory to a God they could not see
Causing blessings and goodness to prevail.

America has been a guidepost for many.
We can't see the whole picture, it's beyond our scope.
Until Jesus comes back and makes things perfect
He provides great strength, endurance and a firm hope.

The Liberty Bell symbolizes our freedom.
The Statue of Liberty stills holds high the torch.
God's special favor still rests on America
Count Him faithful as we celebrate the Fourth!

"The plans of the Lord stand firm forever"
Psalm 33:11

A Holy Day Gift

From the Atlantic to Pacific.
The Sunbelt to the frozen North.
We are reminded of our freedom
As we celebrate July the Fourth

Cod gives us liberty to live
In this land we call our home.
And by His grace He does impart
Freedom the world has never known.

But this gift so freely given
Does not come without cost or price.
For the young and innocent host
Gave up their lives in sacrifice.

God gave us inalienable rights
When this land of our forefathers found.
Take off your shoes America,
For you are standing on holy ground!

The Ultimate Freedom

In 1776 we received unalienable rights
Not a gift to enjoy without vigilance
Nor handed to us on a silver platter
But, to guard and fight for with diligence.
Long before the Magna Carta was granted
Before the Constitution was thought of.
Before the Bill of Rights was written,
God gave eternal rights as proof of his love.
He was always aware of our neediness
And to all who believe on the Lord Jesus
Life, Liberty, and Pursuit of Happiness.
Are fully realized as "In God We Trust."
Real life is found only in serving the Lord.
Liberty is being set free from sin,
Happiness is ours when we pursue Jesus
For true living can only come from Him!
With confidence let us salute the flag
Remembering from whence our freedom comes.
Unalienable rights are ours because
It was God who fought for America and won.

It's for Freedom

To put it plainly and very succinctly
We got our freedom because of God's goodness.
It is nothing we have done it's because of the Son
And not because we were all sinless.

He wanted to deliver us from tyranny,
Wanted a nation who could govern themselves.
So he chose the U.S. and now look at our mess,
Worshiping other gods called ourselves.

Let every flag and parade remind America,
"It's for freedom we've been set free."
Let's fight for the right and proclaim the light
Please, God, arouse us from our lethargy.

God hasn't forgotten you America
You are his jewel in the midst of the turmoil
It's the last days, be ready to be amazed.
Miracles will happen for evil is already spoiled.

Our Flag Is Still There

I love America, it's the
Home of the brave, land of the free.
To quote the eloquent words of
Author Frances Scott Key.

No land has been more blessed
For our cause has been just.
We have acknowledged God
And in him we still trust.

It's for freedom we fought
And in adopting this land
We pledged our allegiance
And united we shall stand.

There'll always be battles
It's the price we must bear.
But we can look up and see
that our flag is still there!

Liberty throughout the Land

I love the Fourth of July, don't you?
With outdoor picnics and the ants.
Fireworks down on the beach and sand.
The warm weather coming at long last!

Families gathering in the back yard.
Grandpa on the couch pretends he's awake.
The ice cream, hot dogs, barbecue and games.
Cake from a box like mother used to make?

I love the celebrations and what they mean,
From the rolling hills to waving golden grain.
From the great skylines to every village green,
Freedom still rings and liberty does still reign.

I hope that we'll always remain young in spirit
Remembering the heritage that's ours alone.
To pledge allegiance to this great country
And each makes freedom a choice of their own.

God is still in love with America!
It's a jewel set in His own resplendence.
With His precognition, at the precise time
He gave us the Declaration of Independence!

Dear Lord...

For every moment I live in this land.
For many blessings that come from your hand
I am grateful to you my Lord, and my God.
Your grace and glory I humbly applaud.

As I consider this liberty I enjoy so much,
And knowing protection comes from your touch,
Teach me to love your precepts, your cause,
To stand up for the good, speak up for your laws.

Let me not go to sleep and close my eyes,
And ignore the obligation and duty of mine,
To pray for all those who have taken a trust,
Who get lost in politics' abyss of power and lust.

Forgive us, Lord, we've lost much in transition.
Thinking more of self and our human ambitions.
Bring back your power, shine your bright light
On the blackouts that obscure your face from our sight.

Hear my plea, Father, redirect all our paths,
Painful though it may be to fool your divine wrath.
Change us, God, so we can bring you great pleasure
Let America, once again, be a land you can treasure.

The Declaration of Independence

The Pilgrims set sail for the New World
Ignoring hunger, exposure and disease.
Half of them died the first winter
Being bereft of any comfort and ease.

God had a purpose in their misery
Sad sacrifices had to be made.
A high price gives everything value.
In pain the path of freedom was laid.

It's easy to take for granted
This mighty show of God's grace.
This jewel of our inheritance
Others struggle for in our place.

History testifies to our journey
With many lives crushed and torn.
From tyranny we won the fight and
America, the beautiful, was born!

Mission Accomplished

Queen Isabella arranged for a voyage
And chose Columbus to carry out her plan.
She wanted to find new routes to the orient
To transport goods easier by sea than land.

Sailing in three tiny ships on a vast sea
On an ocean none could measure or sound.
Some thought Christopher would fall off the edge.
But God knew the earth wasn't flat but round.

He found a land of Indians and wild beasts
Not the ultimate aim, and not worth much money.
But God's timing was perfect, when all was ready
This would be the land filled with milk and honey.

A century had flown by and at just the right time
The persecuted ones came travel weary and worn.
Because they fled their lands in order to serve God
America, the Majestic, was conceived and born!

Labor Day

Labor Day

God calls us to His vineyard
There's a harvest yet to gain.
The crop is ready for gleaning
Ripened by warm sun and rain.

The ground has been prepared
By those laboring in their day.
Tilling the soil and planting,
Obeying the call, working the clay.

Many are those who have toiled
Not seeing much fruit or reward.
But when the Gospel was preached
Were willing to follow the Lord.

Souls are waiting to be gathered.
And He who makes all things grow
Has caused the seed to germinate
And we'll reap where we did not sow.

God calls us to His vineyard.
The labrers are few.
The fields are ripe to harvest
And those souls are waiting for you!

A Labor Day Rest

There is a rest for the children of God.
None enters who go their own way.
Abraham received the promise because…
He walked by his faith every day.

He turned from all of his own desires.
Selfish ambition had no claim on him.
He simply believed what the Lord said.
So God moved him from Ur up to Canaan.

He was able to please God immensely.
Experienced power over defeat.
He avoided many problems in life
Making his walk with the Lord so sweet.

There is a land that is promised by God.
Waiting for all who will travel his way.
The land has already been purchased,
The full price already paid.

There is a rest for the children of God.
Where the milk and the honey tastes best.
Self interests, there, are all put aside
For all who would enter that rest!

God's Laborers

Adam and Eve messed up the garden
If my memory serves me right.
They ate forbidden fruit
And day was plunged into night.

They thought God was just kidding
He said, "Don't eat of this one tree."
But he meant it and here we are
It's a struggle for you and me.

But God remembers all the laborers.
They're like soldiers in the ranks.
The "little" people of the country
Conquer their battle without tanks.

They plant crops and build houses.
Some work in factories and homes.
Facing the beauty, pain and drama
Of living life…sometimes all alone.

God sees the struggle of the masses
And their stanch endurance over time…
And all the faithful in his vineyard
Will reap the very best of the wine!

A Labor Day Reminder

The Lord is pleased with workers who consent to
Assume the role of a willing servant.
An act of worship Jesus took upon himself,
Whose work and life was a ready sermon.

You may not have the job of your wildest dreams
A big Honcho of some great firm,
But God is interested in what you are
Rather than what you do and what you earn.

You have been created for his service.
And in love he monitors you and leads
So when the going gets to be too much
He carries you to make sure that you succeed.

It's essential to have daily sessions.
It's a family run business, I might add.
He's the CEO of heaven and earth
But it's our priviledge to call him Dad.

As sons and daughters we must stay in touch.
Nothing could interupt Jesus' prayer time
For the cost of doing business is high.
He recognized a Son needs a Father full-time.

In His Vineyard

Labor for the Lord with all joy and praise.
Serve him with fervant anticipation
Let no gloominess descend upon you.
Fill your heart and soul with adoration.

You know that your labor is not in vain.
Capture all your thoughts, don't let them adrift.
You've been given many abilities
Open your eyes, see your God-given gift.

When your head spins and the world moves too fast
Maintain your balance, change your point of view.
You're working for the Lord not mere man
He's your boss and He's looking out for you.

He's able to make work more palatable.
We are all partners with him on his team.
If he can change the water into wine
Then he can change skim milk into cream!

A Father's Promise

I love the scenes of Autumn.
The change is refreshing to me.
The struggle of summer and fall
With a hint of winter to be!

Many leaves are turning colors
Still others await their demise.
Some trees will give up their green.
None of their foliage will survive.

The nourishment from the tree.
No longer flows from its breast.
And divorcing summer progeny
It sheds its leafy green dress.

God planned it so we can learn,
He gives us beauty beyond reason.
Nothing stays the same for long
And everything has its season.

Summer may be on its way out,
But high on God's promised list
Is the beauty that's totally Autumn
And Indian Summer her kiss.

Good Bye Summer

Autumn is just around the corner and
Out of the womb of summer comes fall.
Seasons will continue to be birthed
For the Father has ordained it all.

Indian summer may pay a brief visit.
Breathe deeply and take one more sip
While the unusual weather lingers
And bestows a warm and fleeting kiss.

Geese will fly south for the winter
The ground will grow lifeless and cold.
Flowers hang their heads in mourning
The frost makes them listless and old.

The leaves begin to lose their green.
Exploding with yellow, gold and red.
They fall to the ground in glory
Making a rich mulch for their bed.

We each experience our own summer.
But there is a time we must all let go.
There is adventure in every season
And comfort even in the winter's snow.

It's Fall!

Warm days are drawing to a close.
Indian summer tries to deceive.
But wintry blasts are coming soon
And earth gets ready to receive.

Leaves fall like wounded soldiers
Drifting silently to the ground.
Nestling with their dead companions,
Feeing earth with their rich compound.

Trees give up their green summer dress
And keenly attuned to autumn's call.
They begin to look stark and naked
Getting ready to sleep, it's fall!

Each new season holds a promise
And keeps an appointed tryst.
A solemn vow God has given...
Earth will never cease to exist.

Thanksgiving

Thanksgiving Virtue

Who hangs the sun and the moon on nothing?
Who speaks to the stars and bids them stay?
Who keeps the planets from colliding
And who gathers up the Milky Way?

Who gives life and breath to all creatures
When, if he wished, he could take it away?
Who allows seasons and time to continue
Unfolding into the years, months and days?

It is the one who wants us to prosper.
Whose blessings are lavished upon us all.
Atoning for sin in the Garden,
Dying in our place because of the Fall.

Let's feast with a heart of gratitude to God.
Reflect on the reason for this holiday.
As we remember his cornucopia of grace
Celebrating it for what it is.. a Holy Day!

Our hearts should overflow with gladness
Not only on this our Thanksgiving Day.
But in all the year with our whole being
Giving him worship and praise everyday!

Dear Lord

As Thanksgiving day comes once again
I thank you for your love so ardent
Meeting my needs and some of my greeds
Enriching my siritual garden.

Help me to be mindful of your mercy
Your cornucopia of blessing so grand,
For ushering me into your presence
When I feel lost and can't find your hand.

Thank you for your family and friends
Bringing glimpses of heaven above
Even though discordent times may come
You weave us with the cords of your love.

Thank you for your Son, Dear Father,
You sent him to die for my sin
I was helpless to save myself
From the enemy's pit I was in.

You made me to walk close by your side
And love and glorify you, God
Remind me not to wait for one day
To give you not much more than a nod!

Give Thanks to God!

Give thanks to God for where you are
And for everything you have
To stay drowned in pain and pity
Is to turn God's good to bad!

Each strange and puzzling experience
Will bring you closer home,
Will mature, settle and mellow you
As you travel the unknown.

Take heart, dear friend, you are not alone
We sojourn this world together
With God your guide and advocate
Your load will feel more like a feather.

Thankful?

In those special times of year
When families gather 'round,
To stuff their tummys full of food
And talk about "those pounds."

They celebrate thoughtlessly
And don't remember why,
The big concern is where and when
To put that piece of pie.

They forget to count their blessings
But remember to appear
At such a feast and gorge themselves
While others starve in fear!

In the time and freedom God allows
They live their lives in satiation
And in their self-centeredness
They offer no appreciation.

They close their eyes and cannot see
God's pockets are so full,
He blesses even though they
Don't act the way they should.

Being thankful is like paying rent
On this earth and all its treasure
And expressing thankfulness and love
Bring our separate worlds together

A Season of Thanksgiving

Thanksgiving Day is here to enjoy
With aromas of delightful smells,
The kitchen warm with hustle and bustle
And family working out small details.

Getting caught up on all the news
Cousins and aunt and uncles meet,
Too excited to stop their play
The little ones can hardly eat!

I love to hear the conversation
To hear the chatter of the clan,
The air full of anticipation
Talking over the holiday plans

It makes me think of that day when
Christ will come and we shall share,
In the marriage supper of the lamb
After our meeting with Him in the air!

Happy Thanksgiving, Lord

God, can we talk about something?
I hope you can straighten me out
I'm unhappy and discontented
Is this what life's all about?
Can I complain about the weather?
Last year there wasn't enough rain
Everything just curled up and died
Will this coming year be the same?

Forgive me Lord for my complaints
I'll get my equilibrium back,
As I concentrate on your goodness
And not on what I want or lack.

You do supply my absolute needs
While people in other lands wait,
For a ship that never comes in
While mine is on time, never late

Thank you for listening, dear Lord,
I'm making my goal holy living
With you to guide me in my life,
We'll both have a Happy Thanksgiving!

Happy Thanksgiving

Ho, hum, it's Thanksgiving, is that how you feel?
You see, gratefulness isn't always automatic.
Life can be exciting, stressful or dull,
Yet, God, unlike us is very systematic

Here's the plan: Everything works together
It all produces fruit while we wait and stew.
God expects us to choose to be grateful,
It's our part, being thankful is up to you.

Cooking in his oven can be painful.
But even a turkey does get cooked through
It can be poked and basted in the process
Then comes out of the heat ready to view.

He never holds back, He gives a big helping
Of mercy and grace to help through the haze
What will your attitude be for your day
As the curtain opens and you step on stage?

Thanksgiving isn't limited to The Day.
It's a worship, a prayer a hymn.
God has made his choice for our lives
Put into motion by our obedience to Him.

I'll Always Thank Him

Christmas may be the time to be jolly
But thankful never goes out of style
To be grateful to God who is highest
Always gives him a reason to smile.

Our hearts should well up with worship
In appreciation of what he has done
For our treasure is not in this old world,
But in what God has done through His Son.

We may say the grace over the turkey,
With such great piety over the food.
But are we really aware of what he does
And how His love flows out for our good?

Our love depends so much on the weather
If our money's safe and health strong
Emotions come and go like the tides,
When Thanksgiving should always be our song

His unfailing love has changed my life,
Now, He is my own special friend.
In every circumstance what ever comes,
I'll thank Him over and over again!

Thank You, Lord

How long will it last, your Thanksgiving?
Is it only a day then it's past?
Are you waiting for turkey and trimming?
For things that never will last?

Do you thank your heavenly Father
For things such as family and friends?
Not just on the day of Thanksgiving,
But as each day begins and ends?

Are the things of life growing stale?
Is it a chore for you just to survive?
Well, begin to thank God for His goodness.
And your interest in life he'll revive

Make each day a day of Thanksgiving
No day should differ from the rest
Look up with a heart full of love
And he'll give you His very best!

Mr. Turkey

I'm glad I don't have to raise my own turkey
Knowing of his demise in the end
I'd cringe if I had to use the axe
While looking into the eyes of a friend.

I can easily mangle the veggies
To butcher them gives me no start.
I can peel, chop them and cook them
With a cold insensitive heart.

With pleasure I'll smother the sweet potatoes
And cover them with butter, sugar and spice
And give them a shove into the oven
To bake them is my joyous delight.

But I can go to the store and buy the bird.
That way I'll never feel any remorse
I'll cook it with a clear conscience
As I only had to make a choice.